100 Minutes of Inspiration
Copyright ©2011 Helen Valleau

Title ID: 1466428570
ISBN-13: 978-1466428577

Email: helen@ayearofpossibilities.com
Website: www.ayearofpossibilites.com

Design by: Yuriko Zakimi at Design With Purpose Inc.

This book is dedicated all my clients and community for your encouragement and precious feedback over the years. I deeply appreciate your desire to achieve greatness for yourself in your life.

I especially want to acknowledge Glori Meldrum for gently nudging me into bringing my Weekly Inspirational Minutes together in book form.

Thank you Yuriko from Design With Purpose for your beautiful design of this book.

Thank you to my family, friends and Spiritual Community, The Centre for Spiritual Living Toronto and The Hoffman Process, for your unconditional love and support.

I find Helen's 100 Minutes of Inspiration, quick, in-a-nutshell capsules of instantly useful, life-affirming, personal-path brightening, and life-direction re-aligning Monet. Yes, Monet. The fuzziness in my life, often looking like an impressionist painting, clears. I shift internally, realigning with true soul purpose and consciously chosen life-purpose fulfillment.

Frank Westcott: Author, 1st. Place Co-Winner Exile/Gloria Vanderbilt Short Fiction Award 2011 for my story The Poet

100 Minutes of Inspiration is a powerful way to begin your day. Each reading inspires you to live your vision, embrace gratitude, and know with your whole being that the universe is always there to support you!

Barbara Burke Author of "I Am Divine"

Helen is a Wisdom Teacher who offers gentle guidance in these inspirational pages whatever your spiritual path, religion, or background. There is sure to be something in this beautiful book that you will recognize and connect with. She offers magical words you can use to shape new thoughts and beliefs…and create something better not only for yourself, but ultimately for the planet itself.

Deborah Hall, Founder and CEO, Calm Today

Helen is a gifted Spiritual Healer. Her latest book "100 Minutes of Inspiration" is yet another extension of the wisdom and love of this talented woman… The book is full of powerful and precise principles easily absorbed and executed into one's daily life.

Lynda Visosky

Helen Valleau has been there for every step of my personal transformation, serving as my life coach and mentor. During this time, I've come to appreciate her as one of the most beautiful, compassionate, loving, and wise people I've ever known. I feel truly blessed to have her in my life, and I'm certain that after you've read 100 Minutes of Inspiration, you'll understand why.

Glori Meldrum, Founder and CEO g[squared] and Little Warriors

As a lighthouse firmly rooted on solid ground, 100 Minutes of Inspiration provides focus and clarity to help navigate the ebb and flow of daily life. Helen Valleau's work is clear and potent; a guiding light that steadily reminds, invites, and inspires one to live on purpose and with purpose. A powerful tool.

Judi Bechard, The Clearing Experience

Read any page of 100 Minutes of Inspiration and you instantly feel empowered by Helen Valleau's sound wisdom and solid advice. She is a powerful teacher.

Trish Orwen, journalist

Lessons learned from Helen Valleau

Love yourself unconditionally
All your power is in this moment, now
You can be anything you want

Helen and I began working together on her first book, **A year of possibilities**. She came to me with the idea of creating a workbook that would require people spending just five to ten minutes a day creating action steps to move them toward their vision. The book came to life beautifully, as Helen envisioned that it would, and it now sits on my nightstand. Opening this book is the first thing I do every day.

As a business professional, it's an honor to serve clients like Helen. The lessons learned working through this process were amazing. Helen walks her talk in everything she does. She lives a truly authentic life. Hers is a life of purpose and passion. She has a deep desire to share all of this with as many people as she can.

100 Minutes of Inspiration is a beautiful follow up to **A year of possibilities.** It is easy to use and it provides us with another great tool to inspire us and move us daily towards our vision.
Thank you Helen!

Love and Light,
Rhonda Page, know your difference

"You are not here merely to make a living. You are here in order to enable the world to live more amply, with greater vision, with a finer spirit of hope and achievement. You are here to enrich the world, and you impoverish yourself if you forget the errand." Woodrow Wilson

Author's Message

Having a vision for your life is like having a compass that sets your life in motion on a journey that you are consciously choosing. Not having a vision, sets you up to live your life by default and then wonder how you got to where you are. Have you ever asked yourself the questions, "Is this all there is to life?" Or, "How did I end up here?"

We are always creating, whether we are aware of it or not. Why not be conscious and present in our lives and choose thoughtfully what we desire to experience? Why not live a life of purpose and passion instead of getting life by default?

Having a vision for your life is not about acquiring all the things that you think will make you look impressive to the outside world. A vision is about connecting to your power within and experiencing a feeling of fulfillment, passion, and purpose, and contributing to the betterment of your life, the lives around you, and, therefore, the world.

The Law of Cause and Effect is always in action. We are the cause of what happens in our lives. As well, we experience the effects of

our choices, thoughts, and actions. Why not make conscious, healthy, and loving choices that impact our lives in a positive way?

This book is designed to be a simple and easy reminder of how powerful and effective you can be in your life by creating a vision, taking conscious action steps, and changing old negative thought patterns into new positive ones. This is not new information. These are the principles of life from the Old Masters such as Buddha and Jesus as well as New Thought teachings from Thomas Troward, Ernest Holmes, Ralph Waldo Emerson, and many others. I have simply packaged these principles into short readings that can be absorbed easily. I am humbled by every lesson for I too am on a journey. I am profoundly grateful for these teachings.

 I wish you many blessings on your journey of consciously creating your life.

Love and Light,
Helen Valleau

When creating my vision, I remind myself of the four steps I take daily to manifest all that I desire.

1. I align myself with the infinite power and goodness of the Universe.

2. I take daily action and do what is most valuable and loving for me each day.

3. I express my gratitude for all that I have that is loving, abundant and challenging in my life. I express my gratitude for all the gifts that come my way as I manifest my vision.

4. I let go of the "How," my vision manifests and I open myself up to receiving greatness!

The beautiful thing about your vision is that you bring something beautiful to the world!

When you are living your vision, you are on purpose and an inspiration (in spirit) to others. It changes your perception of yourself. Living your vision shifts you to a place of empowerment where you can feel differently about yourself and create your life from a place of what's authentic and important to you.

Remember the example of the oxygen mask in the airplane. Use the oxygen mask on yourself first, so you can show up filled with your own loving energy to live your vision. Once you have achieved that, you will be capable of supporting others on their journeys

You may then contribute to the world in a way that is meaningful and for the highest and best good of all. What action steps are you taking today towards your vision?

I focus on what I can do today and affirm each step of action with loving kindness.

In our minds, we are often thinking of what went wrong in the past or what could go wrong in the future. We are not living in the present moment. Allow yourself to be present. Focus on what you can do today and embrace the task with love and kindness. There is only this present moment, and if you are living in the past or in the future, you miss out on the valuable information of the NOW!

Each action step that you take with loving kindness towards yourself, or someone else, creates more love, more positive energy in the future. It may not be apparent to you at the time, yet know that the Law of Cause and Effect is always working. What this means is that the action you take today and the energy you bring to the experience has an effect on yourself, others, and the world, later today, tomorrow, next week, next month, next year. Be clear on what your intention is with each action step you take.

Choose love and kindness and enjoy the outcome!

In this moment, I choose to be present and grateful for all that I have NOW

The present moment is all that I have. The past is over and the future hasn't yet arrived. The only time is now.

By being fully present and embracing this moment, I experience life to the fullest. I am open to receiving all the information that the Universe has for me, and this will guide me to the next moment of presence and the moment after that.

Gratitude is one of the most important states of being when we want to manifest our vision. When we are able to experience gratitude for what may feel like the most difficult moments in our life, we shift our consciousness from a place of powerlessness, to feeling powerful. When we are in a state of gratitude for the experiences that have shaped our life – for better or worse – we move away from what we created in the past and become clear about our desires for the present.

We have an incredible power within us that connects us to the unlimited potential of creation in the Universe. When we are in the vibration of gratitude, this empowers us to connect with our magnificent power within and manifest all that we desire.

I have faith that all my dreams and desires will manifest.

To have faith, means to have a firm mind, even in the presence of difficult and trying moments.

If I have a dream, a desire that I am committed to manifesting in my life, I must hold firm to it in my mind, body and spirit! For when I hold firm in my mind what my desire is, despite any difficulty I am experiencing, I am creating the form for the Universe to bring my desires into existence.

Faith is unshakeable and places us in the position to command and demand goodness as we take action towards our vision.

The more you have and experience faith, the deeper your faith will become, and the deeper it becomes, the more it feeds itself. Soon your experiences will reflect your faith.

**My actions do not create success or failure.
My actions create movement towards my vision.**

So often, we judge ourselves and the outcome of an experience
as a success or failure.

If we can release our judgments and realize that the experience is
a divine opportunity for learning and growth, we will not give up
on ourselves and on our dreams. When we allow ourselves to
be fully present and let go of our attachment to the outcome,
we stay focused on the bigger picture – our vision.

Know that the Universe is always saying, "Yes," to our thoughts
and beliefs. Therefore, if you are thinking you are a failure, the
Universe will reflect your thoughts and say, "Yes, you are a failure!"

If you are thinking, "This is a challenge and I will learn and
grow from this, and I embrace this experience with dignity and
grace," the Universe will say, "Yes!"

There is an infinite flow of unconditional love and positive
energy available to us when we say, "Yes!"

My desire to accomplish my vision deepens my impulse to be of service to others.

As I am living my vision and reaching my goals, a momentum of positive energy is created within and around me. I align myself with the power of the Universe. This is the energy that supports me in living a life that is purposeful and meaningful. From this place of abundance within and around me, a desire to be of service becomes a motivating factor in achieving and living my vision.

To be of service means to add value to your life and to the lives of others unconditionally and from a place of love. It is this act of unselfish giving that fills the heart with joy. Joy is often considered the secret to a fulfilling inner life. By doing for others, we do profound good for ourselves.

Be sure to ask someone today, "How may I be of service to you?"

I embrace the difficult moments with grace and openness to learn more about myself.

In life, there are always difficult and trying moments. The same applies when creating your vision. Some days it may feel like nothing is working and there are numerous roadblocks that prevent you from moving forward. The gift in all of this is the awareness and understanding of how you handle these moments. Do you give up, push yourself to exhaustion, beat yourself up, and blame yourself or others?

This is a divine opportunity to be present, breathe, and let go of control. Surrender and embrace what is, with dignity and grace. Connect to your divine essence within and allow yourself to be guided from within to what is most loving and supportive for you.

You will become clear on what your next action step is. This is a divine opportunity to realign yourself with your purpose, your passion, and your reasons for creating your vision.

My purpose is soul driven; it is my mission in life. It ignites a passion in my heart that inspires me to create my vision.

When we create a vision that is purposeful and soul driven, we are in integrity and unity with our mission in life. It is something that we feel so deeply passionate about that we can almost taste it. It sparks our imagination and creativity that is our life-force energy. Our purpose inspires us to take action despite any difficulties that arise. No one can deflate our vision. We must create it!

I can feel excited and joyous about many experiences in my life. I can enjoy and delight in all that comes my way. Yet, when I am living both my purpose and my mission, I can also endure the difficult moments and continue on my journey of creation. I embrace these difficult moments with dignity and grace and stay true to my vision. This is how I can stay motivated and take action over a long period of time and not give up.

**My thoughts are of giving and gratitude.
I acknowledge all I have accomplished, knowing
I then create a reality that reflects abundance.**

I contribute to the season of Thanksgiving by taking into account all that I have given and received over the last year. Gratitude aligns me with a high vibration of energy. The more I acknowledge what I am grateful for, the more I attract people and experiences into my life who are joyous, loving, and supportive of my vision.

There is no lack in the Universe. But by thinking there is lack, we create lack, and we can always find evidence to prove we are right about that.

The most important thing to understand is that what we are thinking about is reflected back to us. So consciously practice gratitude and you will experience an abundance of giving and receiving.

Practice gratitude by placing your hands over your heart. Breathe into your heart space and acknowledge what you are grateful for today.

I choose to take a leadership role in my life by taking action towards my vision.

What does it mean to be a leader? To lead, means to inspire, which means, being in spirit. I choose to take action daily towards my vision and by doing so; I set an example for others. I inspire others to also step out of their comfort zones and allow themselves to be led by spirit.

The Universe is always creating, always evolving for the highest and best outcome for mankind. When we stay small and fearful we contribute to the collective consciousness that there is something to be afraid of and we stagnate our growth. We are actually going against the current of ease, grace, and manifestation. Life becomes difficult.

Are you waiting for someone else to be first? You be first! Lead the way, set your goals and take action daily. You will be amazed at the support that flows your way because you are evolving with spirit.

My desires first start with a thought that creates my intention. My intention creates a tension within me. This intention is a call to action to support me in creating my vision.

Often we have a thought about something that excites us, but we do not pay attention to it. Our minds will find a way to rationalize our thoughts and come up with all kinds of reasons as to why it is not a good idea.

When we pay attention to the thought and connect to feelings of excitement, joy and passion, the next step is to create an intention. An intention is a focused, activated thought process shaped by our consciousness. An intention puts our thoughts into motion.

From this place of energized tension, take your deliberate action step for today and align yourself with the power of the Universe. Let go of attachment to the "how." It will all happen. Focus on what you need to do right here, right now.

Allow yourself to be open to receiving support from unexpected sources.

What is your action step for today?

**I consciously choose my thoughts and actions
and I expect great results.**

When I am paying attention to my thought process and I am
aware of what I am thinking, I can then choose to shift any
negative thoughts to positive, loving ones that support me in
taking positive action. As a result of taking positive action,
I expect great results.

If I expect anything less, I receive less.

This is how the law of attraction works. The Universe is
impartial; it does not choose who can receive and who can't.
The Universe always says, "Yes!" to what you desire. If you are
unconscious of what you are thinking, then you are unaware
of what you are asking for and most likely not receiving all
you desire.

Choose to focus on what supports you in creating your vision.

Take action on what is loving for you. Expect great results
and you shall receive this abundance.

I release any fears and doubts about creating my vision. They have no power over me.

Often, when we are stretching ourselves into the unknown and expanding our consciousness, our negative thinking can kick into overdrive and take control. It is then easy for us to come up with all kinds of fear-based reasoning and rationalizations as to why we shouldn't continue taking action.

The more power we give our negative thoughts, the more they expand and create our reality.

Each time you become aware of this negative thinking, consciously negate it by saying, "These fears and doubts have no power over me. The truth is that I am infinite potential and possibility and I have the power to create my vision and live a magnificent life!"

Remember fear is the opposite of LOVE. Where love exists, there can be no fear. What do you most need to love and nurture within yourself today?

Each day, I consciously choose positive thoughts that support me in living a magnificent life.

What do you focus on each day when you awake? If you focus on all that is wrong or not working, then that is what expands for you during your day. Say to yourself upon first waking: "Today is a beautiful day, today I am focusing on all that goes well, and today I will allow all the blips to roll off my back."

Everyone experiences difficulties during their day. But it's the people who consciously choose to focus on what is going right for them who will succeed in creating a magnificent life.

Yes, today is a beautiful day!

I am creating a life of abundance for others by living on purpose and in abundance myself.

When I am living my purpose and consciously creating abundance for myself on all levels; emotionally, spiritually, intellectually, and physically, I contribute to the collective consciousness of abundance for others on a global level.

Often, we are not aware that our thoughts affect others. When we are thinking that there aren't enough resources, enough love, enough support, enough of anything, we are contributing to a mindset of poverty consciousness.

Shift your thinking and knowing to a new level. Believe there is enough on this planet for everyone. By doing so, and creating and living in abundance consciously and with gratitude, you contribute to raising the consciousness to abundance for all!

I embrace the difficult moments on my journey with grace and I stay true to my vision.

As part of the creative process we run into roadblocks that can be perceived as negative. The more we stay grounded and connected to our purpose for having our vision, the easier it is to accept that roadblocks are an inevitable experience on our journey. These roadblocks provide a tremendous opportunity for growth.

Our challenge is to stay present and focused on our vision and let go of attachment to the outcome of how our journey unfolds. There are many routes to the same outcome. Sometimes we are so attached to what our route is, that we are unable to see another that may be more supportive in the long run.

When challenged, connect with your purpose for creating your vision. Ask yourself, "How is my vision a true reflection of who I am and what I have to contribute to the world?"

Never be willing to compromise on your vision! If you do, you will inevitably get less than what you compromised on. When you are true to your vision, abundance is created on many levels and you receive much more than you ever could have imagined.

I am in the present moment accepting my life as it is now and I feel the conviction of my desires and vision that I choose for myself.

By being in the present moment and in a place of absolute acceptance and gratitude for all, I am aligning myself with what I desire. If I am focusing on what I don't want, I get more of what I don't want. When I accept what is, and find gratitude in each and every situation for what I can learn from it, I am then able to choose clearly what I desire.

In presence and gratitude I make a clear choice for myself about what I desire. I am definite, specific, and concrete and feel the conviction within myself. I then take action from this place of alignment and presence. I let go of the "how," and expect great things!

Presence, acceptance, gratitude, and conviction = manifestation.

I have faith in the manifestation of my desire.

One of the most important ways to manifest your vision is by having a burning desire. It is the starting point of all your achievements. Desires are not hopes and wishes; they are definite in their nature and fuel a burning flame within that ignites passion and purpose.

This passion we feel is the force of life that propels us to take action until our desires become fact and our reality. Desire, supported by faith, pushes all negative chatter aside in the brain and inspires us to continue on our quests.

Hold your desires in your mind, see them, feel what it feels like to be living your desires each and every day. You will then be inspired to take action and make your desires your reality.

The wisdom of the Universe is mine to tap into any time I choose.

The Universe is here to serve us in creating anything we desire at any time we choose. When I look around and see how much abundance the Universe provides, I am reminded that I have the power to tap into its wisdom and empower myself to create my life the way I desire.

When I realize I am one with the creative intelligence of the Universe and I allow myself to be fully present and in the moment, I receive the perfect guidance filled with wisdom that supports me in creating my life with ease, joy, and grace.

By focusing on what is positive and magnificent in my life, I create a positive, magnificent life.

What we think about and focus on comes about. When we focus on the negative, we attract more negativity into our lives. Often it is amplified. When we focus on what is positive, and how magnificent life is and how magnificent we are, then that is what becomes amplified in our lives.

All of what we think about becomes emotionalized. That means that the feelings that we attach to our thoughts, which vitalize and energize our thoughts, soon begin to translate themselves into a physical reality. Therefore, I choose to focus on, and be grateful for what is magnificent and abundant in my life

My desires and my emotions of faith and passion create a magnetic force that attracts an abundance of positive energy and support for me to create my vision.

When we are in harmony with our desires, our energy vibrates at such a high level that we attract people and experiences into our lives that support us in ways we never could have imagined.

This is why it is important to write out your desires and spend time daily visualizing. Soon you will be living these desires and connecting to what it feels like to be living them. This deepens our faith, which is the basis for all the miracles and mysteries of life. Then we may shift our perception from, "I am powerless to, I AM POWERFUL!"

I choose be loving, kind, and gentle with myself. I fill up with self-love first so that I have the ability to be fully present for others and myself with authenticity, grace, and dignity.

One of the most challenging aspects of staying focused in creating our vision is remembering to be loving, kind, and gentle with ourselves. If we are not filling up with self-love, we run out of fuel to continue taking action.

Filling up our emotional bank account consistently is vital for sustaining faith that we can create our vision and believing that we are worthy of doing so. Often, we wait for others to fill us up first.

I say, "You be first!" Take a leadership position in your life by treating yourself with love, kindness, and gentleness.

I am consciously choosing to complete all the tasks that I start, so I empower myself and continue to take conscious daily action towards my vision.

Persistence, concentration, and a willingness to continue to take daily action, despite any resistance that comes my way, will give me a sense of accomplishment and empowerment that adds fire to my desires.

Often, people give up when the experience feels difficult. This is the time to continue following through and completing what you started.

If you give up, it is like you stop watering and tending a seed that has been planted in the soil. You may not see the seed germinating beneath the soil, and yet if you stop watering, the seed will dry up and wither away.

Have faith that your desires will become your reality because you are committed to taking action.

This is your amazing life to experience. Dream big!

What dreams have you had for your life that you have put on a shelf or negated by saying, "That will never work, it's a crazy idea, and I couldn't possibly create that in my life?"

Anyone who has manifested greatness started with a dream that became his or her vision. Your vision ignites a burning desire within and a powerful momentum is created to propel you to live up to your highest potential and manifest your dreams.

What are you dreaming about today?

Awaken yourself to your unlimited potential.

As creative, intelligent beings, we have the ability to wake ourselves up and become conscious of our unlimited potential to create and live magnificent lives.

By expanding your mind, being fully present and in the moment, versus the past or the future, you have the ability to hear and experience the wisdom of your inner self, your essence. You will then tap into creative solutions that your intellectual mind could not have figured out.

Experience the magic when you let go of figuring out the "how," and open yourself up to receiving greatness.

Open your eyes and heart to all that you have to be grateful for.

When I stand in this present moment and I open my eyes to the beauty, abundance, and glorious creations all around me, I give thanks for all my blessings.

Giving thanks and feeling and expressing gratitude sends a vibration of love through my heart, my entire body and out into the world.

Allow yourself to be open to receiving, for the Universe is an abundant giver and likes to be acknowledged and appreciated.

Honesty, integrity and authenticity are all qualities I choose to embrace on my journey in awakening myself to my purpose and passion.

I choose to share my ideas, beliefs, and what is true for me, even if it is not always what others want to hear.

When I am honest, authentic, and acting with integrity I can choose my words thoughtfully, consciously, and lovingly. I respond to situations with grace, trust, and dignity.

Often, I may feel like the odd person out. Yet in my experience, my commitment of staying true to myself always reveals a deeper connection with my Spirit and what brings me joy in my life.

I embrace each present moment on my journey, and therefore I experience life to the fullest.

All of my experiences are neither good nor bad; they just are. It is when I give these experiences emotion, energy in motion, that they become what I perceive them to be.

I always have a choice in how I choose to respond to any situation. That, too, is neither good nor bad. The question is, "Am I willing to take full responsibility for my response and the consequences of my choice?"

When I am present, awake, and aware, I can embrace each moment knowing that it is a human experience I am having and that on some level I signed up to experience the full banquet of life.

I embrace my magnificence, knowing I am powerful and I have a divine purpose to share with the world.

Today I choose to embrace all of my magnificence and brilliance that I earnestly bring forth into my present experience. I am embodied Spirit that is eternal and powerful. I acknowledge my purpose for having this human experience.

How may I serve? What brings me joy? What ignites my passion? Perhaps a relationship with someone, being a parent, having a deep connection to the Divine, creating and expressing beauty, bringing joy to others, a fulfilling career?

Our purpose gives us a direction in which to focus our intentions so that we are in a constant state of creation and evolvement for the highest and best good of all.

The more you embrace how magnificent you truly are and love yourself in spite of any perceived flaws, the more you will discover your divine purpose.

I focus on what I can do today and affirm each step of action with loving-kindness.

In our minds we are often thinking of what went wrong in the past or what could go wrong in the future. We are not living in the present moment. Allow yourself to be present, focus on what you can do today and embrace the task with love and kindness. There is only this present moment, and if you are living in the past or in the future, you miss out on the valuable information of the NOW!

Each action step that you take with loving kindness towards yourself or someone else creates more love, more positive energy in the future. It may not be apparent to you at the time, yet know that the Law of Cause and Effect is always working.

What this means, is the action you take today and the energy you bring to the experience, have an effect on yourself, others and the world later today, tomorrow, next week, next month, next year.

Choose love and kindness and enjoy the outcome!

In this moment, I am present and grateful for all that I have NOW.

The present moment is all that I have. The past is over and the future hasn't yet arrived. The only time is now.

By being fully present and embracing this moment, I experience life to the fullest. I am open to receiving all the information that the Universe has for me. This will guide me to the next moment of presence and the moment after that.

Gratitude is one of the most important states of being when we want to manifest our vision. When we are able to acknowledge gratitude for what may feel like the most difficult moments in our lives, we shift our consciousness from a place of powerlessness to a place of feeling powerful. When we are in a state of gratitude for the experiences that have shaped our lives – for better or worse – we move away from what we created in the past and become clear about our desires for the present.

We have an incredible power within connecting us to the unlimited potential of creation in the Universe. When we are in the vibration of gratitude, it empowers us to embrace our magnificent power within and manifest all that we desire.

I have faith in my ability to manifest all my dreams and desires - my vision!

To have faith, means having a firm mind and the strength to continue taking action even in the presence of difficult and trying moments. Faith without action does not allow us to create.

Committing to a vision for my life means holding firm to this desire in my mind, body, and Spirit! For when I hold my vision firm in my mind, I create a container for the Universe to bring into my existence all that I desire.

Faith is unshakeable. It places you in a position to command and demand goodness as you take action towards your vision.

The more you have and experience faith, the deeper your faith will become. The deeper it becomes, the more it feeds itself, and the more your experiences will reflect your faith.

Change is constant. Life is always evolving.
I know that all my experiences have a
beginning and an ending. The space in between
is where my vision is realized.

Nature demands change so that we may evolve in consciousness.
Change is the constant. We are creative in nature and always
evolving towards our highest and best good. Being able to
embrace change rather than fighting it or fearing it, allows us
to experience a state of grace.

Endings allow us to let go of what doesn't serve us. The Neutral
Zone is the place where our new vision is realized and we can
make sense of past hurts. The Beginning is the place where we
embody a new way of being and become inspired to take action.

Wherever you are on your journey, accept and embrace it
knowing that change is imminent.

My journey in life brings wisdom and self-awareness. I embrace every opportunity to live joyfully in the expansion of self-discovery and transformation.

There are times when we cocoon to regroup and rejuvenate ourselves. Then there are times when we feel bursts of creative energy that bring about growth and expansion. By staying present to the journey wherever we may be, we may experience the wisdom and joy that is our birthright.

Joy is our natural state of being. But sometimes, as we struggle in the trenches of transformation and evolution, we forget this natural state. Be sure to take time each day to laugh, play, and delight in the simple pleasures of life. Your heart will be filled with joy and gratitude.

I have a compelling desire to serve and inspire others through manifesting my vision.

When creating my vision from a place that resonates deeply with my spirit, I ignite my passion for being present to all of life's possibilities. I know I am living on purpose and aligning myself with the infinite goodness of the Universe.

Living with purpose and passion launches us on a joyful and creative journey that inspires us to follow in seeking what is truly possible in life. To inspire means to be "in spirit" – connected to your divine power within. It is from this connection that you evolve in consciousness and serve the highest and best good.

Through manifesting your vision, you will move beyond the focus of acquiring external things. Yours will become an inspiring, joyous, loving, life journey.

Love is your true nature, your true power. Love is an intention that can inspire you to live authentically, and in peace and harmony with yourself and the world.

When we have the desire and intention to put love first in our lives, miracles happen.

By being loving, kind, and gentle with ourselves first, and then to others in our lives, we illuminate the truth of any situation. Love is intelligent. A mystic knows this truth and experiences love in all things. A mystic knows this from the heart, not just the intellect because the power of love is the fundamental principle of our existence. We need love in order to thrive. Being loving is our inherent nature.

Something powerful happens when we are filled with love. We are able to bring this love to any difficult situation. Love inspires our work, our creativity, our relationships, and our well-being. Love can hold and cradle us during the painful times in our lives.

Remember to breathe into your heart and connect to the abundance of love within, for that is the truth of who you are.

My desire to accomplish my vision deepens my impulse to be of service to others.

As I am living my vision and accomplishing my desires, a momentum of positive energy is created within and around me. I align myself with the power of the Universe.

This is the energy that supports me in living a life that is purposeful and meaningful. From this place of abundance within and around me, a desire to be of service becomes a motivating factor in achieving and living my vision.

To be of service means to add value to your life and to the lives of others, unconditionally and from a place of love. It is this act of unselfish giving that fills the heart with joy.

Joy is often considered the secret to a fulfilling inner life. By doing for others we do profound good for ourselves.

It is co-operation versus competition.

Be sure to ask someone, "How may I be of service to you today?"

Along my journey towards my vision I will experience some difficult moments. What I know for sure, is that within those moments there are gems of information for me to learn and grow from.

Our journey is never what we expect or anticipate. There are always moments of delightful surprises and angst-ridden questioning. Often we may ask, "What was I thinking? How did this happen?"

When we can embrace and enjoy the delightful surprises, it will give us the strength to walk through the difficult times with dignity, grace, and an openness to ask this fundamental question: "What can I learn from this experience?"

We can find gratitude for this learning and this will empower us to continue taking action one-step at a time.

I honor my body, mind, and Spirit by ensuring that I take loving care of all parts of me.

I cannot separate one part of myself from another. For Instance, what I feed my body affects me energetically and therefore mentally. How I nurture my Spirit affects the energy of my body. The thoughts that I think and the feelings I feel affect my body and spirit.

I am worthy of the holistic commitment to self-love and self-care. Doing this allows me to meet my own needs rather than expecting others to do so. This is how I ensure that I remain in integrity. Honoring my body, mind, and spirit empowers me along my journey.

Like attracts like, and so I stay focused on my purpose and what I desire in my life. The Law of Mind is in perpetual motion. What my mind holds within, becomes form in my world.

My ideas determine what I will create in my life. The mind force is continually creating. Nature does not differentiate between a seed, a weed, or a flower. Whatever I plant and focus my attention on, will grow.

If you are planting seeds of fear, replace them with love and courage. If you are thinking limited thoughts, replace them with thoughts of abundance, knowing that you are connected to a source within the Universe that is infinite in its potential and power. You have the ability to create your life any way you choose by planting the seeds that are right for you.

To be living my vision and gain all that I desire, I must first ask the following question: Are my thoughts controlling me or am I controlling my thoughts?

I know negative thinking that dominates me, or makes me a servant to what it dictates, will delay any good that is coming my way. If I am using my thoughts for gains, I am on the path to creating my vision. If my thoughts are using me for continued loss, I am putting obstacles in my own way.

Mother Nature follows the Law of Order and Discipline. If our minds work in an orderly, disciplined and constructive way, then we have the power to create our vision. All action is the result of thought and I choose to use thought to gain the best that life has to offer.

When I realize my desires, it instills within a devotion to learn, grow in consciousness, and experience even more of all life has to offer. Life is abundant, and I am never satisfied with one state of being.

The Law of Good is Universal and always advancing for the highest and best of all mankind. Each day when I focus on all that is abundant and beautiful in the world, I also expand my consciousness of the infinite goodness that is available to each and every one of us.

If I focus on lack and worry about what is missing, I restrict the flow of abundance. This will drag me down into deeper fear and worry. It is not about all the things I possess that make me abundant; it is my consciousness, my state of mind. For what I focus on, expands.

What are you focusing on today?

I know that my desires, without the expectations of their manifestation, are idle wishing or dreaming. I command great outcomes for myself and expect nothing less!

When I earnestly define my desires, I set up a force of positive energy within that connects me with the invisible energy of my desire. I create an "intention - in tension."

My intention is useless unless I expect to receive my desires in part or in full. Continuous expectation is necessary in order to bring my desires into reality. Be careful. Never expect something you do not want and never desire something you do not want. You are very powerful and you will manifest all that you desire and all you expect.

Know that you are worthy of manifesting your vision and expect nothing less than anything Divine!

Each day I spend five minutes focusing on what I desire. Feeling calm and peaceful, I create a mental picture in my mind. There is a quiet conviction within me that knows what I seek will come to me.

The clearness and strength of the mental picture in my mind of all I desire to create brings a knowingness that I am on purpose. By taking action and doing what is right in front of me to do, I will create a channel for manifestation.

Creative Intelligence operates within you. You have the power to access this knowing. Amazingly, it enables you to manifest all that you desire to round out your life and make it fuller and happier. Of course by doing so, you contribute to the well-being of others and this makes the world a better place.

Interest - Attention - Expectation Simply focus your attention on all that you are interested in creating for your life. Expect and anticipate its manifestation for it is yours to experience any time you choose.

What is it that you are most interested in creating and experiencing in your life? What really excites and ignites a flame so bright within your soul that you are willing to intensely focus your attention on it? What can so consume your mind that anything that is petty or selfish is absorbed by a higher interest and your desire to live consciously, honestly, and authentically is fulfilled?

When we charge our interests so firmly with the knowing that there are no failures and expect success, there is a magnetic attraction that takes place and brings our interests into form.

We can then expect only to achieve.

I embrace the attitude of giving. I am in alignment with the fundamental law of life. This is the first Law of All Creation.

Giving unconditionally from a place of love is a way of being in service. When we give our best, that serves to better the world. When we give our best without concentrating on returns, we experience that our purpose and prosperity become blended.

I choose to concentrate on the joys of giving versus concentrating on what I feel entitled to get back. This is not careless, impulsive giving. Think of giving in a careful scientific manner that is responsible and supports the highest and best, therefore yielding a great return.

I am the architect of my life. I build my vision step by step and stimulate all the good within. Therefore, each day I praise myself for every action step I take.

By continuously praising myself, I transform positive energy into active force. Having faith in my vision promotes understanding and wisdom. By praising myself, I am also consciously applying my understanding that I am powerful and capable of living a life of purpose and passion.

Lift your consciousness to a higher realm. By praising your efforts, you open yourself up to receiving all the goodness that is waiting for you to experience. On a physical level, the cells of your body strengthen. Praise can also change your perspective, for you can look for the accomplishments and the good and beauty that is yours to have.

When I learn to take what I have and build upon it with praise and gratitude, I align myself with the principles of the Universe.

Even when I think I don't have much to begin with, I start in action and praise all that I do have and experience. As a result, I open myself up to receiving much more. I get more than what I expect and when I declare my desires with the energy of praise, joy, and thanksgiving, I am expanding my consciousness of abundance.

When we are thankful in advance for all that we are expecting to receive, this is an expression of our faith in the present and our vision to come. It is also powerful to praise in the face of adversity so that we do not become a victim to circumstances. To have the power to praise, even in our darkest moments, will unfailingly force the light to shine through.

**When I am in fear, it feels like a hologram
filled with substance. Then when I go beyond
it, fear feels like an illusion – false evidence
appearing real.**

The definition of a hologram is a three-dimensional image
reproduced by a pattern of interference. Fear is a pattern
of interference that can feel all encompassing and real.
By giving into fear, I prevent myself from moving forward
towards my vision.

Fear is a double-edged sword. It can set off our inner alarm
bells saving us from real harm, or it can simply talk us out of
doing something new and exciting.

Next time a fear shows up that would prevent you from moving
forward, remember to breathe, focus on what you desire,
acknowledge the fear and do it anyway.

I have a compelling desire to serve and inspire others through manifesting my vision.

When creating my vision from a place that resonates deeply with my spirit, I ignite my passion for being present to all of life's possibilities. I know that I am living on purpose and aligning myself with the infinite goodness of the Universe.

Living with purpose and passion is a joyful and creative way to inspire others to reach for life's infinite possibilities.

To inspire means to be "in spirit," connected to your divine power within. It is from this connection that we serve our own highest and best good, both for ourselves, and for others.

A vision is not about all the external things that we might acquire, it is about the feelings of joy and love we experience on the journey of creating our vision. Our vision has the power to inspire others to live in love and abundance.

There is a silent process forever working through me, all around me, carrying on all of the unconscious activities of my body without any effort on my part.

My subconscious mind holds all the memories and experiences of my lifetime just below the threshold of consciousness. What I experience in my life is a result of my conscious and unconscious beliefs. It is the expression in the concrete of my mental equivalent.

As I examine my relationships, health, career, finances, and my own personal growth, I consciously replace old thought of lack with a new, bigger, and expansive idea. I do this by thinking quietly, constantly, and persistently about what I most desire. I am clear and definite about what most holds my interest.

Know that you live in a mental world, that your thoughts become expressed through you and you experience your life exactly according to your beliefs. Whatever enters into your life is the expression of what you believe consciously or unconsciously.

The first step to creating consciously is by being clear and definite about what I choose to be rid of - ill health, financial loss, an uninspiring job, a relationship that is unfulfilling. I let go of the belief that this is how my life has to be.

Next, I get clear about my desires and what interests me most. It is the polarity between my desires and my interest that activates my emotions. This dynamic energy propels me into action.

I think it, I feel it, and I get interested in it, and I take action. That is how the mental thought becomes expressed in the material world.

"Why do we need a vision," you ask? "You thought visions were for the fairy and unicorn people?" It is your duty to have a vision and demonstrate love, abundance, and harmony in your life.

The Law of Being states that we are creative beings here to express life to the fullest. If you are not creating, then you might as well stay in bed or take a stroll to the nearest undertaker. To express life to the fullest is to demonstrate that there is a Universal goodness that is omniscience, omnipotence, omnipresent and omni-active.

If you desire to change your life, if you desire to be healthier, happier, vital, and more prosperous, then you must have a clear vision of what you desire to demonstrate. Doing this allows life to flow through you with ease, joy, and grace instead of happening to you by default.

What do you desire to demonstrate in your life?

How do I create a new reality for myself?
I must change my thinking and keep it changed.

It is so easy to shift out of negative thinking when we are in a positive atmosphere, when we are with like-minded people or when we are listening to an inspirational speaker. It is easy to say, "Yes, I can do this!"

Yet when we go out into the world and get on with our lives, we can easily forget all about creating that new reality with positive thinking. In order to succeed, stay focused on your positive thoughts. Be aware of how you feel when you are thinking positively. Also, be aware when negative thoughts enter your mind and don't let those thoughts take over.

Change your thoughts and keep them changed.

By focusing on what I desire versus what I don't want in my life, I create a mental equivalence (think of it as a mental container) for this desire to become my reality in the material world.

I must ensure that I am clear about what I desire without being overly specific and attached to when and how it happens.

By creating a mental equivalence of your desires, you are saying to the Universe, "Yes, I am ready to receive this into my life and have this experience!"

When you furnish your mental equivalent, providence moves too. You will experience so much more than what you dreamed of in the ordinary way.

That is the power you possess within!

Shhh…I hold my vision close to my heart and contain it within me. This is vital, for I do not wish to dissipate the energy building around my vision by having other people's opinions influence me.

Everyone will have an opinion about your vision. Some will love it and others, because of their thinking, will find ways to discredit your vision. The moment someone isn't as enthusiastic about your vision as you are, your bubble may burst, especially if you are the type who looks for other people's approval.

By containing the energy, it allows the flame of your desires to build into such a strong light that it dispels all darkness and negativity. You will shine so bright that no one can dispute your vision.

I shine my light on the inner ghosts and goblins of my past. As I shine my light into those dark places, I realize that they are not as scary as I once thought.

One of the biggest hurdles in creating a vision is bringing the past into the present. The past no longer exists except in our minds. When we stop plugging into the past, thus making it still valid in the present, we free ourselves and give ourselves fully to life.

All those stories we tell ourselves create a veil over the truth. And the truth is that we are spiritual beings having a human experience. We forget that we are here to love, and be loved, and have a joyous time, not to continue to beat ourselves up.

Let go of the past, be in the present and remember that you are perfect, whole, and complete. You are not broken.

Allow love to live in every cell of your mind and body.

The definition of insanity is doing the same thing over and over and expecting a different result. Sooner or later I must be willing to change my thinking and master my negativity to experience my desired goals and vision.

We all have destructive habits in our thoughts and behaviors and some are eroding the quality of our lives more than others. It is not about being perfect; rather it is about being authentic, realistic, and loving.

When you decide to implement change, it is important that you have others in your life to support you on your journey.

The unconditional support of others is most valuable. Of course you are the one who still must take action each and every day to change. The best part is this; YOU have the power to do it!

Each day I set my intention to do my work and tasks to the best of my ability which inevitably brings out the best in me.

Granted, my best is different each day as each day brings about different circumstances, feelings, and energy levels. What I know for sure, is that when I maintain my intention of doing my best, there is a sense of satisfaction at the end of the day.

Each time I choose to do my best, I increase my ability to do my best and there-by attract better and better circumstances and results into my life.

Think of it as giving yourself a blue ribbon at the end of each day.

In the morning, instead of hitting the snooze button, I activate my energy by standing up and speaking an affirmation that supports me in starting my day.

How often do you hit the snooze button and roll over hoping for few more minutes of peaceful sleep? What happens is that those few moments are just enough time for all the negative chatter to start up in your head. That means that fear, doubt, and worry are getting a jumpstart on your day.

Create a positive affirmation that makes you feel powerful and enthusiastic. Then when your alarm rings, throw off the covers, stand up, and state your affirmation. Do this for 30 days and you will have created a new way of starting your day.

My home, office, and even my car are a reflection of my ruling mind. If these places are in disarray, cluttered and dirty, then most likely my thought processes are cluttered, and it is difficult to take action towards my vision.

In order to create more, do more, experience more, and attract more abundance into my life, I must first clear the clutter. I let go of all that does not serve me emotionally, mentally, and physically. I put into circulation anything that can be used by someone else with gratitude for when it was of use to me.

I create an orderly, beautiful, and open space for goodness to come into my life. Yes, I do this on all levels, emotionally, mentally, and in my physical space. It really is the little things that count. If I don't take care of and honor all that I have now, then how will I be able to take care of anything new that is bigger and better?

Make de-cluttering a lifestyle.

I let go of blaming others or circumstances for any difficulties I may be experiencing in creating my vision.

Somewhere in my subconscious thinking there is a snag. Ouch! "You mean it's me, not them?"

Yes, we reap what we sow and this is, believe it or not, mathematically accurate. If I attract something that doesn't feel good, it is because of some dormant belief that is to be awakened within me and released. This is happening so that I manifest something better for myself.

When I sustain my ability to constructively use the experience for my own evolution in consciousness, I can release what doesn't serve me, knowing the goodness that is then available to me is limitless. There is a simple saying, "I let go and let God. And so it is!"

Oh…all that chatter in my mind prevents me from staying focused on my vision. I call it monkey brain. Those cheeky monkeys start to fill my head with all sorts of nonsense to distract me from being focused on my goal and taking action.

This is when I say, "Blab, blab, blab," give my head a shake, take a deep breath, and say, "Thanks for sharing, now STOP IT!" I refocus my thoughts, to ensure all that wishy-washy chatter does not mar the demonstration of my goals.

If you focus on your goal and take action for a month, you will be astonished at the results.

Of course the first action is to open the door inwards towards your soul. This is where beauty, magic, and passion live; this is what fuels true action towards manifestation of any goal or desire.

As part of the human condition, I know that I carry within me false beliefs about the world and myself. It is these false beliefs, conscious or unconscious, that keep me imprisoned in some form of lack.

We all grew up with a belief or two about how the world "should" be or how our lives "should" be.

These beliefs can be a prison for remorse, lack, pain, resentment, unintelligent fear, or illness. We believe that circumstances keep us in that prison.

The truth is the door is always unlocked and we are free at any time to choose a life that is limitless, a life filled with love, abundance, health, and prosperity.

The hardest part is taking that first action step to turn the handle and open the door and walk towards your vision.

In each area of my life, my relationships, my career, my finances, my spiritual growth, and my health, I praise the goodness that is evident. I say with conviction out loud, "Life is wonderful! I am grateful for all the abundance that is mine to give and receive!"

Gratitude is vibrant and active. Look at all the areas in your life and acknowledge all that you are thankful for. The more you praise, the more you receive.

Having the attitude of gratitude is not enough. You must be active and participate in the energy so that you create more of what you desire.

Today, consciously participate in blessing, praising, and giving thanks for all of the abundance in your life.

I stop fighting with myself and realize that true peace of mind does not come from discord. It is only by surrendering, accepting, and embracing what is in this moment versus resisting, that I am able to open up to peace and harmony.

If I believe I have to work hard or overcome some sort of limitation, then all my attention is on working hard and on my limitations. I focus on my goal, embrace each and every experience with the knowing that this is presenting itself to be removed, and I open myself up to limitless possibilities.

This is the Law of Non-Resistance. It is only by me being Non-Resistant, in acceptance, that I can focus my thoughts on what is most helpful and supportive to me.

Energetically I am in alignment with all that is good for me. When I am in alignment, I open myself up to receiving all I desire.

Of course, whenever I embark on a new journey, it can at first feel difficult. Sometimes it seems like there are too many obstacles in the way. If I take each obstacle, and see it as a challenge and opportunity for growth, the obstacles become blessings and I am triumphant.

It's so easy to get bogged down in looking at all the challenges when we start something new. It is always hardest at the beginning.

But the depth of knowledge, understanding, and awareness gained, is priceless.

When you change your energy from being powerless, overwhelmed, and fearful, to that of feeling powerful, anything is possible.

Tell yourself the following; I will learn all that I need to. I will learn from my mistakes. I will bless each difficulty with the energy of love and gratitude.

By affirming these positive thoughts, you will feel empowered. Your faith in your abilities will deepen, and you will be filled with hope for a better life for yourself and those you love.

Sometimes I feel too busy and that I have too much to accomplish in too little time. When I look at my agenda and feel overwhelmed, that is a good time for me to ask myself the question, "If I am not saying NO to what ultimately doesn't serve me, what am I saying, YES to?"

It is so easy to get caught up in saying yes to everyone and everything for fear of not being liked. Perhaps you feel it is selfish to say no and put yourself first?

I attract what I expect and if I believe that I must put others before myself then I will attract others who will demand this of me. When I start to put up healthy boundaries and say, "NO," even if the other person doesn't like it, I will start to attract people who have a sincere desire to see me put myself first and succeed in my goals.

Being a doormat for other people to dump their baggage on does not create space for you to take action on your dreams.

Start expecting others to take responsibility for their lives and you take responsibility for yours.

Ask yourself the following question; "Are my conversations with others uplifting to myself and the other person, or are my conversations filled with complaints?"

Have you ever noticed the content of your conversation? Is it filled with complaints about yourself, your day, your life, or others, or is it filled with inspiration, passion, joy, and love?

This is something to be aware of, for you may automatically complain without being conscious of what types of conversations you are participating in.

Take the time to think carefully about the intention behind what you are speaking. Be aware of what you are feeling emotionally and energetically. Most of all, create conversations that are loving and supportive. This will activate a much higher level of vibrational energy within you, and as a result, you will have more energy for creating your vision.

I know I am authentically empowered when I naturally create harmony in my relationships. I am authentically empowered when I am co-operative in all endeavors with ease and joy. I am authentically empowered when I experience deep reverence for living life to the fullest.

When I have a need to please others for fear of disapproval or being disliked, I am tense and expecting the worst. The intention to become what someone else needs me to be for him or her disrupts the harmonious relationship with my spirit.

It is a sacred task to do what you were born to do - live your life with purpose and passion. In order to give the gifts of your soul to others, you must first learn to give to yourself.

Set healthy boundaries and learn to say no to what doesn't serve your highest and best good. You will then experience what it feels like to be authentically empowered.

Where I am in this present moment is exactly where I need to be. Do I bless this moment or do I curse it?

I choose to open my eyes and appreciate the beauty around me. I choose to open my ears and listen for the guidance that is always available to me. I choose to open my arms and receive the abundance of support waiting for me. I choose to open my heart and receive the love that is available to me.

Thank you for the blessings of this present moment. Thank you for the blessings of the past and thank you for my future blessings. This is what I choose to focus on. I know that I cannot always control what happens in my day. However, I can choose to bless each moment with gratitude and love. This is where I do have a choice.

What is your choice in this moment?

Success in life is not a destination. Success is the joyful expansion of energy and consistent movement towards the demonstration of my goals. When this is happening, I experience a divinity, a beauty, and grace in all my endeavors. This is the true meaning of success.

So often we seek to define being successful by what we have acquired or what we have accomplished, ensuring that we look good on the outside to those who may be judging us. That is a lot of energy expended to keep up with the Jones's.

What if instead of needing to look good on the outside, we felt good about ourselves on the inside and were unattached to the perceptions of others?

What if we could experience miracles of creation and manifestation every day by shifting our perceptions from those of lack and disappointment to those of abundance and success? What if we could feel such an omnipresence of love and divinity in all that we do? Would we ever again question our ability to be successful?

Know you are divine just the way you are.

I choose not to expend my energy by creating friction through fighting, resisting, and needing to prove I am right when an obstacle presents itself. When I step onto the path of non-resistance I will ultimately reach my goal. It may take a little longer, yet I will have more energy and a deeper faith in my abilities to manifest my dreams.

I choose to take a stance for my dreams, my purpose, my vision, and my highest and best good. Taking a stance for something does not mean fighting against a condition and creating more angst. It does not mean being submissive or a doormat for the poor behavior of others.

Taking a stance for yourself and what you believe in means standing in the truth that you can act from a place of love, compassion, honor, and integrity. As well, it means you can disarm the weapons of fear and hate. We attract into our lives what we believe and expect.

Expect great loving things for yourself and respond accordingly.

Martin Luther King, Gandhi, and Mother Theresa all took a stance FOR what they believed in.

There is a quality that I bring into my life that is as limitless as my faith, love, and desire to create. Forgiveness – for giving life to myself over and over again. Forgiveness also becomes a lifestyle.

"Why do I need to forgive myself and others who have hurt me," you ask?

I choose to arrest my suffering. I choose to stop restricting the flow of goodness from coming into my life. When I am holding grudges from the past towards others and myself, I am the one drinking the poison and hoping the other person dies.

Think of forgiveness like pulling weeds out of your garden. When you pull out all the roots of a weed there is space for you to plant the seeds of your desires. Of course, new weeds might also start to grow, so tending to your garden consistently is imperative.

To truly experience the illumination of my
spirit, I must dissolve all unforgiving thoughts.
When I free my mind of all wrongdoings
towards others and myself, I free my heart
from past hurt and pain.

It is by letting go of past hurts that I open myself up to
receiving new possibilities. If my thought realm is filled with
resentments, (re-sentiments), then I am restricting the flow
of goodness that I can receive in Spirit, abundance, love, joy,
peace, and prosperity.

Make a list of your resentments and take note of how long
you have been holding on to them, a day, a week, a month,
a number of years? Ask yourself, "What am I getting from
holding on to all this bitter energy?" Make a conscious choice
to let it go and be free from this low level of vibrational energy.

Be first in forgiving yourself and others, for it is in the school
of forgiveness that valuable life lessons are learned.

Every desire I have consciously chosen requires discipline and persistence. It may mean constant study, practice, action, and focus, and I am willing to sacrifice what doesn't serve me to embrace what does.

Despite what our humble beginnings may have been, any obstacle can be overcome when we are willing to sacrifice the time, resources, or energy to attain our goals. No one becomes a master of his or her craft without discipline and persistence.

I like this description of discipline: to teach with leaving our dignity intact.

What is it that you need to teach yourself while maintaining the integrity of your spirit and your dignity?

I seek out others who are living their dreams to mentor and inspire me to live mine.

There are many people who have overcome adversity and gone on to become great leaders. These are the people I hold as a benchmark of possibility for myself.

When I look to others for inspiration and higher learning, I expand in my consciousness. This enables me to do more, become more, and create more, and leave behind my fears and doubts.

There are many people in this world who are committed to living on higher ground. This is a place of integrity, honor, dignity, kindness, and love. They may not be yelling the loudest, yet they are out there.

Set your intention to find someone to inspire you to greatness.

I have the freedom to choose what I desire to manifest in my life. Freedom means that I am in control of how I respond and know when to let go of what I cannot control.

When I feel exempt from the control of what others say, do, or perceive, I have the power to determine my actions. I do not need the approval of others. I am free to choose my course of action by listening to my Spirit and my intuition, which will guide me safely and lovingly on my journey.

True freedom is the ability to choose what is most loving and supportive for you despite other people's opinions. Many people will have a judgment about your choice and many people will believe they know the best and right way to do something.

But everyone knows what is best for him or her even though it may look like a mistake to someone else.

Trust that you know what is best for you, and others know what is best for them. You are always free to choose for yourself.

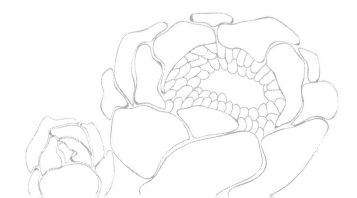

I am a conscious co-creator of my life. I am committed to living my vision. I am ready to shape my experience of life by focusing my attention on the good in my life.

I am living with the awareness that I am consciously co-creating my vision with the Universe. I step onto the path of living in this truth and know that life moves through me. Life does not just happen to me.

I am a full participant in shaping my life. I am in charge of my life. I focus my attention on all that is good in my life, and the goodness expands. I am deeply grateful for all the goodness, and I not only think about this, I express my gratitude, and I praise the goodness.

Oh my goodness! My goodness is more abundant than I ever dreamed possible.

When it feels right to me, that is my truth meter. That is when I know something is good for me despite what others may think or feel.

I listen to my heart and I feel my feelings knowing that my feelings are my ally. They give me valuable information to orient myself in my world.

Your feelings are not your identity; they are energy in motion sending you signals. Learn to identify your feelings, give them a language that encompasses more than, "good, fine, OK, or better." Your feelings are the way you channel your creative energy. Trust them, listen to them, and discover what is true for you.

My judgments of others are a mirror for me. For what I judge in others, is always an opportunity to learn more about myself and what I am projecting out into the world.

What I see in others is a reflection of myself. If I am critical and judgmental of other people's behaviors and characteristics, chances are, they are reflecting an aspect of myself that I really don't want to acknowledge. I react to others by building a case against them in my mind without really knowing the person or understanding what motivates their behavior.

The opposite is true as well. If I put others up on a pedestal and only admire their "good" qualities, and yet I am criticizing and judging myself, I separate myself from my own goodness.

We all have great qualities and we all have aspects of ourselves that we can improve upon. Most importantly, be aware of what you are focusing your attention on and how you perceive others. These are gems of information that can support you in understanding yourself in relationship to others.

I choose to open myself up to new, fresh, and exciting ideas. These are ideas of the future that bring me to a place of greater consciousness, joy, prosperity, and abundance.

If I continue rehashing old ideas, trying to breathe new life into something that really doesn't excite me, I am setting myself up for more of the same. Humdrum ideas just don't cut it. Your thoughts hold a vibration of energy that becomes manifested in your world. If something isn't exciting, interesting, and meaningful for you, then let it go.

Your mind can think up infinite ideas. You can choose the thoughts that bring you joy, that you find fascinating and intriguing. These ideas of the future are your thoughts in this moment, the NOW. By being present to this moment and by being a receptacle for your ideas, you are the inventor of your future.

If I am sitting on the fence about making a decision, since I am just not sure what to choose, I am setting myself up to fail. Having an indecisive pattern can lead to feeling powerless, meek, and fearful, and it can therefore sabotage my vision.

People who are successful have decisive minds and are willing to take responsibility for their choices. You have a powerful mind and you can choose what you think and what you focus on. Not choosing is also a choice that leaves us in the place of being a victim.

Do not let fear of failure prevent you from making a choice. The answers that support your highest and best good are within. Despite what advice others will give you, nobody knows you better than yourself. Every great achiever had a thought that they made a decision to act upon.

What are you waiting for?

Since all of creation starts with a desire, must I then struggle to achieve this desire? Of course not. I will struggle only if I believe that life is a struggle and I must work hard to be worthy of receiving my vision.

It is the subconscious beliefs that life is hard and stressful and that I must strain myself emotionally, physically, mentally, and spiritually to be worthy of receiving, that stand in my way of an ease-filled, stress-free life. Another barrier to an ease-filled life is a collective consciousness that states that if I am not busy all the time, I am actually wasting time.

What you desire in your heart is your greatest asset. The emotion you feel from your heart's desires indicates the experiences you will have when you make that choice to have them. Stay connected to the emotions and the feelings of your heart's desire. This will allow you to create from a place of ease, peace, and grace, despite what is going on around you.

In my darkest moments, when it appears that fear and doubt prevail, I rely on my faith that there is power in the Universe supporting me in my heart's desires. My faith is like seaweed, deeply rooted within, yet bending and flowing with the waves of emotion that fill me.

There are many times when I question my decisions, my desires, and my vision. Still there is one elementary truth that keeps me rooted in my faith. There is a creative power in the Universe, always expanding and evolving, always abundant and filled with infinite possibilities.

The more I step out of my comfort zone, the more that little voice in the back of my head says, "Really? Are you sure about this? Maybe you just want to go back to the way things were? It's easier!" This is when I rely on my faith in the Universe and my Spirit within. My Spirit is the part of me that is eternal, an individualized expression of the Universe here to live a magnificent life! I can choose to rely on my faith or listen to that little voice in my head that says, "Play small."

What is your choice today?

I focus on these five basic fundamentals of learning a new way of being:

1. Who do I listen to? I listen to my Spirit, my essence, first and foremost, and then I listen to the experts. The experts are those who walk their talk and manifest their visions.

2. I stay open to learning. Everyday I ask myself; what is my teachability index?

3. I apply what I have learned. This means taking action daily.

4. I understand the four steps of learning when applying what I have learned. The four steps are: 1- Unconscious Incompetence, 2- Conscious Incompetence, 3- Conscious Competence, 4- Unconscious Competence

5. I MASTER these basics of learning.

I ask myself, "What is my teachability index today? How teachable am I? Am I open to learning something new?" The more teachable I am, the more I will succeed in life.

If I am not open to learning and growing, then I am most likely shutting out valuable information that could help me achieve my desires. In other words, I am shriveling up and dying. How often do I say? "I get it, I get it." My ego thinks it knows it all.

When I am willing to be in a state of consistent practice and openness to learning, then I am getting "it." Getting "it" is not about arriving at a single destination. Getting "it," means being on a continuous journey of growth and experience. I remain open to new ideas and ways of thinking. This makes me teachable.

The best way to get to a place of unconscious competence, to master a new way of being, is by building my mental muscles. I practice focusing my thought processes over and over. I also make it a priority to observe others who have achieved what I desire.

Success breeds success. It is important for me to have a mentor who inspires me to learn and achieve more. It is important for me to stretch myself. Who is walking the walk and who nudges me to be at my best on any journey I embark on?

Yes, I may feel incompetent for a while, and it may feel uncomfortable. But I don't let that deter me. I remain focused on what I am choosing to achieve and I stay open to learning. This is how I forge new neuropathways in my brain and get to the place of unconscious competence, a new pattern of being.

Persistence – Patience - Practice

Each day I commit to my learning by reading books and listening to CDs over and over again. Every time I re-read a book, I learn something new and I master the message being taught.

When I commit to studying a new concept, I must then apply the concept in my life, learn from my mistakes, study some more, and apply the concept again. This is how I become masterful in manifesting my desires.

We must be willing to become the student again. Our ego will tell us that we already know it, "I am an adult, after all. I have life experience." While this is true, our teachability index must always be on high. We must be willing to change, and let go of the "HOW" it's all going to happen. When we apply what we have learned, this is when we experience the magic of manifestation.

By the way, that includes reading these readings over and over!

When someone hurts me and I have a desire to retaliate, I consider the wisdom of the Chinese philosopher Confucius. He said: Before you embark on a journey of revenge, dig two graves.

Where do I choose to focus my energy? Would I rather be right or happy? Feeling righteous can give me the illusion that I am powerful. Feeling righteous can also mean I am reacting against someone else instead of doing what I should be doing - taking a stand for myself.

No one can make me feel inferior. No one can hurt me, shame me, or make me angry unless I consent to it consciously or unconsciously. I have the power to choose how I respond. If I react by having the desire to get back at the other person, I have lowered my vibration to their level.

Today I choose to take a higher road for I know I will then attract into my life others who are living their lives at a higher vibration.

Like attracts like. What are you attracting into your life?

What if I knew I was capable of creating the life I desire and that was ALL that I knew?

Today I make the choice to know and live the belief that I am capable of creating and living my Vision.

If that were all I knew about myself, and I didn't have all those limiting beliefs running my life, I would be creating my vision at warp speed.

The good news is, in any given moment, I can choose to release the limiting belief and be one with the divine power within and all around me. The Universe is omnipresent, omniscience, omnipotence, omni active and limitless in possibility.

When I experience disillusionment along the journey of creating my vision, I must realize the following:

Life is always changing, and the more I embrace change, and the less I fear change, the easier change happens.

My purpose in life is to live in love and joy and to learn and grow in consciousness.

This is it! This is my amazing life to experience and no one is going to create it for me or come along and save me. I am 100 per cent responsible for my life and all that I attract into it.

The more that I acknowledge, embrace, and live from the knowing that I have the power and potential within that I call my Spirit, the more that I will demonstrate in my life all that I desire.

At times, I must renew my enthusiasm for creating my vision. There are those moments on my journey when my life may feel dull and boring, and I may begin to question what I am doing and why.

This is where being disciplined in my life and with my spiritual practice will behoove me. It is important to not allow these dull moments or lack of enthusiasm to become normalized in our way of being.

Take a break, do something that will bring you joy, and most of all, get reconnected to the truth of who you are and the mystery of life. This way, you can experience your Oneness with the Divine that is in you and all of life. This way, you will rekindle your burning desires.

The most important thing I must do when I make a commitment to create my vision is to take action within 48 hours. This will activate the neuropathways in my brain.

If I do not take some kind of action within 48 hours of making my commitment, I am forging neuropathways that tell me, "I am lying to myself, I am a loser, I am incapable of creating my vision." But when I take immediate action, I kick-start my brain into thinking I am capable.

It doesn't have to be a big action step that will overwhelm you. Do something, anything that will confirm to yourself that you are moving forward on your journey.

Remember, successful creators of their vision are always too busy doing what others are still talking about.

Where am I resistant to change in my life? What belief about life or myself am I hanging onto? Where in my life do I put on the brakes choosing to be right rather than happy?

These are all good questions to reflect upon from time to time. It is easy to move into the place of being a martyr or victim. When I wake up and realize that my outer experience is a reflection of my inner thoughts, I can replace these thoughts with ones that will help me develop the willingness to be open and to learn and grow in consciousness.

Be willing to let go of what is causing fear, doubt, pain, or distress. It may feel uncomfortable if that way of being is emotionally familiar. Sometimes, all we need to do is shift our perception of ourselves.

See yourself as capable, open, flexible, changing, evolving, unique, and divine.

Today I discern what is most supportive and loving for me. Discernment is the positive side to judgment. Discernment is a fundamental tool to connect with what feels most loving and empowering for me.

Discernment allows me to be open to exploring my inner journey and feelings and become familiar with my own energetic response. I can recognize what is real and eternal (loving) versus an experience that simply doesn't resonate with me. Judgment is often a reaction to an experience or person that will shut me down emotionally and spiritually.

To discern, allows us to create healthy boundaries and make a conscious choice of what is right for us. This builds our self-esteem and self-confidence. We make choices based on what is in our highest and best good. This is self-loving and self full.

When we are in this state of being, we attract more of what we desire.

Everyday I say, "I do what I love, I love what I do." Life is not about working hard to survive. Life is about being excited and passionate about what I do. The activity in my life reflects this.

If I am complaining, whining, and saying that I have to work hard in order to make a living, then my thoughts about what I do create my reality. Life becomes a struggle.

When I shift from the negative or destructive thoughts to ones of joy, gratitude, and happiness, I become energized and I feel passionate about what I do. The more passion I bring to what I do, the more my life reflects this. Soon, I am living in the sweet spot. The sweet spot is where I manifest my vision while feeling passionate, on purpose, and in contribution to the betterment of the world.

I let go of the time limits I put upon myself, for I know that my vision is manifesting, and I am not attached to when and how this happens.

As long as I am enjoying the journey of creating my vision, for I feel empowered and passionate about what I am doing, the when and how doesn't matter to me. I am living the gratifications of creating my vision and this is how my vision manifests. I feel the feelings before I have consistently created my vision.

This is one of the most important concepts to master when creating your vision. Your job is to enjoy all that you are creating as you follow your journey. This is akin to planting seeds in a garden, then watering and fertilizing them. You cannot predict when these seeds will emerge from the soil and grow into what you planted, but you know that one day it will happen. All you need to do is bask in the sunshine and enjoy the ongoing process of tending your garden.

I know that I know that, I KNOW that whatever my mind can conceive and bring myself to believe, I can achieve. Yes, I become what I think about most of the time.

If I believe in what I am conceiving in my mind, I do have the power to achieve it. In order to achieve my desires, I focus my thoughts and connect to what it feels like for me to be living as if these thoughts had already manifested into my reality.

I focus on this consistently. I practice. I am persistent and patient with myself for I know my mind is very powerful.

It's vital for each one of us to live our vision. When we are living our vision, we are creating life from a place of love, truth, and principle. We are living in the highest and best good for all mankind.

We all have a purpose. We all have gifts to bring to the world. To not fulfill your vision is a travesty to yourself, your loved ones, your community, and the world.

You are valuable, discover your purpose and passion, take action and bring your gifts to the world.

Please visit with Helen at:

www.ayearofpossibilities.com

Sign up to receive a monthly Ezine and Weekly Inspirational Minute in text and audio

Or contact her at:

helen@ayearofpossibilities.com

Other products by Helen are:

A year of possibilities

Create a life of purpose and passion
365 simple action step to make your life a masterpiece

Possibility Movies

A series of Mind Movies to eliminate negative thinking and create positive action in your life

Made in the USA
Charleston, SC
06 May 2013